"You're just a Quote away from your Greatness

Inspirational fuel for your journey

LISA GUICE

This book is a work of fiction. Names, Characters, places and incidents either are the product of the author's imagination or are used fictitiously, and any resemblance to actual persons living or dead, business establishments, events or locals is entirely coincidental.

Farabee Publishing
P O Box 322
Chandler, AZ 85244

ISBN: 978-194478682-3

Library of Congress Control Number: 2016934106

Printed in the United States of America

Book Cover designed by: Allison Denise

I dedicate this book to my wonderful mother Carolyn Payton who despite the fact that she is fighting breast cancer right now has shown me unbelievable strength and courage through this process. You never know what life will throw at you but it is really a true art to make lemons out of lemonade. By her side at the hospital, I wrote this entire book while she received chemotherapy. Our weekly running joke was that "we will have to give a special thank you to cancer for its TEMPORARY presence and assistance in demanding a reason for me to sit down and create this masterpiece". Mommy I Love you and have no doubt that we will both come out on top.

"You're just a *Quote* away from *your* Greatness"

Acknowledgements

I have learned that life is to be lived to the fullest while your **Greatness** is still on fire. You will encounter many who will cross your path but for those who poured into you remember them most. As I am completing the final touches of this book, I cannot help but think about those who have played a major role in pushing, pouring, encouraging, and motivating me to keep going until it was complete.

First, I have to thank my heavenly father for loving me enough to trust me with the gifts and talents I have been blessed with. I also have to thank him for choosing me for my specific journey. Even in the past when I felt unworthy, his love was more than enough to cover me.

To my husband **Shaune** (the love of my life, my high school sweetheart) you are the definition of a good man. I thank you for your sacrifice and dedication to our children and me. Most of all, I thank you for ALWAYS being a supportive husband of my dreams and aspirations. You are my friend, my cheerleader and my backbone. Thank you for allowing me to pursue my dreams and always be Lisa.

To my children **A'Shari, A'Jaune,** and my nephew/third child **Dhymel,** you are all destined for Greatness and the reason I keep going. I know that when you see me running towards my Greatness it is an example of your possibilities. I will always support you following your dreams. Go Get it, I love you infinity (I win).

I must take a moment to mention my little sister **Teara,** and my big brother **Tate** who have both been true examples that it is never too late to go after your dreams. I love you both for the impact you have made on my life, never allowing me to be stagnant and always pushing me to grow.

I am forever grateful to my aunt **Rosalyn,** my sister-in law **Veronica,** and Mother in-law **Gwen** for keeping me in your prayers and going out of your way to share with me how my journey has affected you. You women may not realize it but often your words were the fuel I needed to keep the fire burning. I love you.

My lifelong friend **Suzy Davis** thanks for all the late night talks and allowing me to vent and throw ideas at the wall. Most of all thank you for your honesty when those ideas were less than stellar. I love you girl.

My friend and inspiration **Sierra Rainge**, you came into my life and re-sparked California Lisa (Go Getter-What). Thank you for thinking enough of me to share your journey and dreams with as well as pushing me to live limitless. I thank God for bringing us together.

A special mention is required for **Mr. Gail Bailey,** who told me at the young age of eleven that I was a star and that he would never stop seeing me that way or calling me what I truly am. I am sure he never knew the magnitude of that conversation until now.

I will forever be grateful for my friend **Arnetta Durham.** Your obedience is the reason I realized the calling on my life and left fear for faith. I will love and cherish you always.

A special thank you to my three mentors:

Angela Fort (Founder of Christian Women Business Group), from the first day we met you spoke Gods word over and into me with furry and conviction. I thank you for your guidance and belief in me. You saw things in me I was not ready to see in myself, but that never stopped you from sharing what you saw through your eyes. Thank you for seeing me before I did. (True Angel)

Dr. Will Moreland (Will Moreland International), there is something to say about an individual who does nothing but pour into every person they meet no matter their background, social ranking or economic status. You are the epitome of how to go after your dreams and Live Genius. Thank you for always dropping priceless Genius Jewels on me.

Dr. Vernet A. Joseph (#1 P3 Speaker, Strategist & CEO of Live To Produce Enterprises, LLC) I want to thank you for your boldness. This boldness prompted you to challenge, push and encourage me to write this book. I did not know what I was getting myself into by accepting your challenge but I am grateful that you would not let me squirm out of it. You are a man who walks the talk and I am thankful for your place on my journey. I will never forget your mantra #BeProductive or #BeReplaced.

You're just a
Quote
away from
your
Greatness

Table of Content

Introduction

My life changed the day I began to infuse positivity into my daily routine and self-evaluate. That is the reason I am writing this book. I want you to feel the joy and transformation that takes place when you make the decision to infuse positivity and add self-reflection into your daily routine. An undeniable shift will begin to happen as you embrace all things positive and let go of all things negative. The reality is for many, walking into **Greatness** is something that is unattainable and often just for others. However, that simply is not true. **Greatness** starts with a decision, followed by a belief in you and action to move towards it.

If you are not walking in your **Greatness,** it is because there is a blockage that has occurred and is preventing you from believing you are worthy and deserve it. These blocks are often perpetuated by daily negativity. This negativity continues to feed your already fragile state. Well this stops today.

This books intent is to provide a daily reconditioning tool to help you navigate through the obstacles that stand in the way of you reaching **Greatness Status.** My gravitation to devouring positive quotes started me on my journey to **Greatness.** I used the quotes to push, fuel and inspire me. I used them to debunk all the negativity placed in my head and the loop I had on repeat hearing, "You will never be anything".

The quotes became my friend and lifeline as they would pick me up and reset my hard drive of internal doubt. I quickly realized that quotes were like food to the soul. The more quotes I read the stronger I became. The stronger I became the more I started to recognize my **Greatness.** Once I recognized my **Greatness,** I was now equipped to walk into my purpose. The same can happen for you.

Let's Get Started!

Let No Obstacle Bind Me

Inspirational fuel for your journey

Fear

Please Fail Me Now!

"Fear is the choice to believe in a false truth created by our insecurities."

Our insecurities play a major part in propelling our fears forward. You see, fears cannot grow or take root if the presence of doubt is not already within us. It scares us and manifests itself into a weapon that we use and feed our insecurities like a vicious cycle. Once we acknowledge our insecurities and address them, we begin to start the process of starving fear and removing its power.

Action Toward Greatness (ATG):

Think about your insecurities.

What fears have you created, that you would like to get rid of?

_____

_____

_____

_____

"Fear is only as strong as you allow it to be."

The word fear is really your way of saying you do not believe something is possible. The more validity you give to this thought the stronger your fear becomes. Without your cooperation, fear could not exist because it is after all just a thought. Therefore, when you control your thoughts you control your fear. Focus only on those thoughts that are full of positivity. Starve your fear of its momentum by quickly speaking the opposite.

Action Toward Greatness (ATG):

Today pay close attention to every time fear rears its ugly head. Whatever it says, immediately speak the opposite aloud.

When have you let fear keep you from accomplishing something you really wanted?

_____

_____

_____

_____

"Fear is a thief that will rob you of your destiny."

Just like there are stealers of joy, there is also a stealer of your destiny. That thief is fear. Fear will rob you of the precious commodity called time. It cripples people for days, weeks, months and even years from going after their dreams. If you allow it, it will do the same to you.

Action Toward Greatness (ATG):

Make a decision today; no longer allow fear to steal your destiny.

What have you put in jeopardy of fear stealing from you? (Dreams, goals etc.)

_____

_____

_____

_____

"When left unaddressed fear can cripple the most talented, freeze the most gifted and intimidate the most confident person."

Permitting fear to escalate, can catapult you into a space where you are no longer in control of your ability to move forward in life. This is when fear is at its most powerful and detrimental state, because it stops you in your tracks. Ignoring and giving into your fears can prove to be the worst decision you have ever made in your life. If you are someone dealing with fear, getting a handle on it and facing the root cause is paramount. It is so important to become the ruler of your fear, by developing an immediate way to debunk it.

Action Toward Greatness (ATG):

Practice asking yourself fear-debunking questions.

Is this emotion real?

_____

_____

_____

_____

What insecurity is tied to this fear?

_____

_____

_____

_____

What is the positive I can take away?

_____

_____

_____

_____

Has there been a time when you were frozen with fear (explain)?

_____

_____

_____

_____

Looking back on the incident what are some other ways you could have handled your fear.

_____

_____

_____

_____

You're just a
Quote
away from
your
Greatness

"Fear should never be spoken. Instead speak what you fear as something you are forging, pushing through and conquering."

Life and death are in the power of the tongue. Be cognoscente that what you allow to cross your lips, you are declaring to exists and be true. Do not speak over your life that which you do not desire.

Action Toward Greatness (ATG):

Become mindful of what you say. Practice turning negative talk into positive talk.

I will forge through.

_____

_____

_____

_____

I will push through.

_____

_____

_____

_____

I will conquer.

_____

_____

_____

_____

I will (fill in your declaration).

_____

_____

_____

_____

*Be Fearless

Inspirational fuel for your journey

"If you are brave in your thinking and daring in your actions, you can accomplish anything."

Everyone has dealt with fear. It would be unrealistic to say you will never feel fear again. However, dealing with fear from a brave point of view gives the power back to who should have it, YOU. Be brave enough to think you can and bold enough to know that if you do you will build your confidence beyond measure.

Action Toward Greatness (ATG):

Write down brave and bold actions you can take to overcome your fear.

Name 5 things you will now be fearless about (you must stick to them).

_____

_____

_____

_____

_____

"You will never regret something you've tried but you most definitely will regret not trying what you feared."

Pushing yourself to try something, you have been afraid to do, will always result in a feeling of great accomplishment. There is nothing like being able to look back and say, "I did it". However, allowing that which you fear to keep you from trying will always leave you saying "I regret, I never". In order to avoid an "I regret, I never" life, you have to push through that which scares you. You are actually at your best when you are uncomfortable. That is when real growth happens.

Action Toward Greatness (ATG):

Reflect on a time when you pushed through your fear.

List a time when you pushed through fear. Focus on how it made you feel.

_____

_____

_____

_____

You're just a *Quote* away from *your* Greatness

A Baggage Full of the Past

"A person who has the expectation of getting emotions from someone who is not capable of giving them is a person who has just set themselves up for disappointment, frustration and a life full of crazy."

There comes a time, when we must all come to the realization that everyone is not and may never be equipped emotionally to give us what we are looking or longing for. The truth is, regardless of how much we desire the change; people cannot change something that they do not possess. We are molded and shaped based on our life exposures and experiences. What maybe a natural way to love and expressing love for us might be a draining and unnecessary task for someone else. Ultimately, they do not understand our way of being. It is not for us to dictate the way others should be rather accepting who they are. This acceptance alleviates the stress that comes with looking outside of ourselves to fill whatever void is present. Depending on the wholeness of others rather than focusing on the actual person that stands before us, lays an unfair burden on someone who was unaware that being in our lives meant healing all our issues.

Action Toward Greatness (ATG):

Check your wholeness card.

What is the component that _____ is missing?
(Name the person, what you perceive they are missing)?

_____

_____

_____

_____

Based on who they have shown themselves to be, what characteristics must I be ok with (You decide if those are things you can live with)?

_____

_____

_____

_____

Is there something I am looking for someone else to fix/fill in me (or my life) that I should remedy?

_____

_____

_____

_____

Inspirational fuel for your journey

"When you hold on to the past you are signing up for a life on repeat."

Our past has the potential to replay itself like our favorite song in heavy rotation. **"Holding onto the past is the kryptonite to our future"**. The only thing this accomplishes is holding us down and keeping us from our **Greatness**. It is detrimental to our wholeness, to keep the past around for anything more than a place of reference and learned lessons. Giving it any other space or purpose will result in the temptation to use old memories and pain as a crutch to will ourselves into those same situations, replaying them repeatedly. We run the risk of it becoming the tainted glass in which we see our lives and every situation through. How can we have new dreams and new visions if we are looking with an already colored glass? There is no room for anything new when we are holding on to everything old.

Action Toward Greatness (ATG):

Past Purging

Is there something in your past that you have been holding onto and would like to get rid of (if so what is it)?

_____

_____

_____

_____

How has it held you back?

_____

_____

_____

_____

What was the lesson you were suppose to get out of it and leave the rest behind?

_____

_____

_____

_____

Inspirational fuel for your journey

"Letting go of things that hurt you is a sign that your healing is more important than your pain."

Some are so vested in their past and its pain that they will fight to the grave to keep it (literally). They mention it whenever a situation occurs "You know I had a bad childhood and when you do that I have flash backs".

I call this the **Whinny Bird Syndrome (WBS).** This is when someone uses their past trauma for their negative benefit. Using this to hold off taking personal responsibility for their behavior is typical. They walk around with that mechanism in their pocket, ready to push the button and use it at any glimpse that they are not receiving the sympathy and consideration that they desire. It is fairly easy to recognize this person for they are the ones who say whatever they want to, at everyone else's demise but never want to hear what they've done wrong.

For a female, she is the one who starts to cry the minute you confront her and even appear to have something to say. For the male, he is that person who is so busy yelling and getting defensive that he could not hear what you had to say even if you had a chance to open your mouth.

I am sure we have all encountered people who brandish their past like the weapon they have taught it to be. They are so busy thinking that they are fighting us when really they have masterfully constructed a harmful way to keep themselves stuck in a perilous world of reliving the very thing that brings them to tears. It is not until they get to a point where they desire healing from the past as more important than the benefits they are receiving by holding onto it, that the past and its pain is truly released and forward movement can ultimately take place.

Action Toward Greatness (ATG):

Review your Past Pain

Have you been guilty of using your past/pain as a crutch?

_____

_____

_____

_____

Has holding onto your past issues at times been more
important than your healing (be completely honest)?
Explain

_____

_____

_____

_____

What visions do you see for your life, which can help you resist falling back into old patterns?

_____

_____

_____

_____

You're just a Quote away from your Greatness

"Holding on to the past allows the person who hurt you to have a permanent imprint on your life."

One thing often forgotten as people come and go from our lives is the fact that they only have as much power as we give them. Unless granted permanent residency within our internal hard drive for which we hold the key. When hurt occurs and we allow it to keep us from going after our **Greatness,** we have just allowed the perpetrator of the pain to have a permanent imprint on our lives and future. The same is true if we are allowing the past and its pain to alter our character or personality. That person wins every time we let an opportunity pass us by, stay guarded, do not experience love, or lash out at others because of insecurities established by our past encounters. If we have removed them from our lives, then why allow them to linger in our heads?

Action Toward Greatness (ATG):

Internal hard drive √ check

Who have you allowed from your past to seep into your internal hard drive?

_____

_____

_____

_____

What are some of the lies they have told you that are preventing your Greatness?

_____

_____

_____

_____

Name two things that they said you could not do or be.

_____

_____

_____

_____

Inspirational fuel for your journey

"Just because your past wasn't what you wanted, doesn't mean your future can't be."

Your future does not reside in your past. There is a reason why in order to see the past you have to look behind you. It is something that has already happened which means the best is yet to come if that is your desire. The past is a distant memory in comparison to what your current and future **Greatness** has in store for you. Instead of allowing, the past to hold you back why not use it to your advantage. Take all the lessons and strong emotions and use them to catapult you into your future destiny. "You cannot change what was, but you can certainly write what is to be."

Action Toward Greatness (ATG):

Pull from your past

_____

_____

_____

_____

What from your past, can you look to as
inspiration/motivation?

_____

_____

_____

_____

What dreams were crushed in your past? Are they still
passion triggers for you?

_____

_____

_____

_____

Rewrite the dream/vision in its original form (before it was tainted).

_____

_____

_____

_____

You're just a *Quote* away from *your* Greatness

A Pledge To My Past:

I will no longer allow you to dictate my future or keep me from my future dreams, visions, and **Greatness**. Whatever your hold was on me, no longer exists after today. I am aware that you are powerless unless I fuel you with my voluntary submission. Today in this moment, I am leaving you behind and reclaiming the power over my head, my heart and my destiny.

Signed: My past does not define me.

You're just a *Quote* away from *your* Greatness

Inspirational fuel for your journey

To Know Me Is To Love Me

"People always want to know how much you love them. Why is it that no one ever thinks to ask how much are you loving you?"

All of your life you have been programmed to focus on everything outside of yourself. It is completely acceptable to give love however, do not dare expect to receive more than you give. Truthfully speaking it is impossible to give love if you do not know what it means to love yourself. This is asking you to give away what you do not have. You must experience love first hand in order to recognize it when you see it and know it when you feel it.

Action Toward Greatness (ATG):

Be loving and gentle towards yourself today. Share a time when you should have loved you more than you did someone else (i.e. in a relationship, or other situation).

_____

_____

_____

_____

"How I feel and what I think about myself becomes the example the world uses when deciding how to treat me."

We are the mirrors that reflect to the world our self-worth. No one in this world comes with a written manual, so our rulebook is created by how we treat ourselves. Just like an object we possess, an outsider can determine how much we love and appreciate it by our actions. If we abuse it or neglect it, the world can pretty much surmise that we do not really care about that item. The same is true when we put ourselves down or allow others to treat us badly. The world will follow our lead.

Action Toward Greatness (ATG):

Practice treating yourself better.

_____

_____

_____

What message are you giving the world about how to treat you? (be honest)

_____

_____

_____

"Self-esteem is like the foundation poured to build a house. If it's full of cracks, the structure built on top of it will eventually fall and have to be rebuilt again."

It is natural that over the years our self-esteem may have experienced a few bumps and ended up with some cracks in the foundation. The danger comes when we move on without repairing those cracks. Unfortunately, when this occurs it means we have left them to spread and weaken us. As with anything weakened there will be a breaking point and our job is to repair the broken before we break.

Action Toward Greatness (ATG):

Self-esteem evaluation required.

Has your self-esteem suffered from multiple cracks? (If so, what are they and what needs repairing.)

_____

_____

_____

What steps do you think you can take to start that process?

_____

_____

_____

_____

"Develop a picture of yourself that only holds you in high regard and you will rise to the occasion."

The higher you think of yourself the more your subconscious will try to become the picture you have painted for it. Your subconscious will begin to take pride in that very elevation and look to it as a guide of who you are to be. Imagine what you could become if you could be anything you picture. That is what you are creating. A hand held obtainable portrait. Put yourself on a pedestal and do not let anyone knock you off or move you. **NOT EVEN YOU.**

Action Toward Greatness (ATG):

Visualize a picture of you in the best possible light.

_____

_____

_____

_____

Write out what your picture of your best you would look like? (do not hold back)

_____

_____

_____

_____

"You are a work in progress but the majority of your work needs to be dedicated to getting to know and love EVERYTHING YOU."

We should all have and keep the mindset of constantly progressing in life. Our main desire should be getting to a place where we cherish whom we are and love who we are to become. As long as we are moving forward, we should never doubt that we are capable of the ultimate love, which is self-love. Loving and knowing who we are releases an unspoken feeling within. That feeling is the feeling of personal freedom.

Action Toward Greatness (ATG):

Focus on EVERYTHING Great about you.

Make a list of all the wonderful things about you.

_____

_____

_____

_____

_____

_____

"When you define who and what you are, it leaves no room for the world to have a say so."

If allowed the world will try to mold and alter who you are. It will label and box you into its definition of what the best you should be. Do not allow any wiggle room. Take control over your story like an author writing a book. The world cannot edit what it has not been given access to or what has already been published.

Action Toward Greatness (ATG):

What picture does the world have of you?

_____

_____

_____

_____

Who are you? (you should be able to describe you with words)

_____

_____

_____

_____

Who do you strive to be?

_____

_____

_____

_____

Inspirational fuel for your journey

"Don't let anyone be the author of the story you were given the pen to write."

You have the gift of being able to be anything you want to be in this life. Although you cannot control all things that happen, you can control how you perceive it. As well as how you bounce back from it. When you give your power away to others, you are allowing someone outside of you to alter your destiny. You are handing your pen over to them to write and tell your story which leads to them controlling your future. It is your life; treat it as a blank canvas that is waiting for your Greatness to unfold.

Action Toward Greatness (ATG):

Think of a time when you allowed someone else to have control over you.

Share that time.

_____

_____

_____

_____

Rewrite this time with you staying in control.

_____

_____

_____

_____

_____

_____

_____

"You're just a Quote away from your Greatness"

"Anything negative that you have on repeat is to be purged from your mind with swift and deliberate force."

The mind will play and rerun all negative thoughts that you allow yourself to think. This will be counterproductive to moving forward and walking into your Greatness. The only solution is to purge these thoughts from your mind daily. Imagine how efficient your computer would remain if you took the time to clean its hard drive on a daily basis. The more negative space freed, results in more room for positivity. **Now let's get free!**

Action Toward Greatness (ATG):

Think about what negative things you have said about yourself.

Purge the negativity through visualization.

1. Find a quiet space.
2. Sit in a comfortable position.
3. Think of a negative word you have thought about yourself.

Visualize (close your eyes so you can see the word).

    a. Grab that word out of the air
    b. Squeeze the word tight in your hand until it crumbles
    c. Take 3 deep breathes
    d. Open your hand
    e. Blow the crumbles out of your hand
    f. Keep your hand open
    g. Visualize a piece of paper with a word opposite of the negative word landing in your hand
    h. Visualize writing your name on the paper with the word
    i. Continue to visualize the paper with the word and your name. Say out loud I am _____ (fill in) 5 times
    j. Take 5 deep breathes and open your eyes

Now do not stress if you had to open your eyes to follow the steps. As you continue to practice this exercise, it will become second nature to you.

What you are doing is destroying the negative thought and replacing it with a positive thought through visual and verbal reinforcement.

After a while, this technique will become so second nature that you will be able to visualize positivity and destroy negativity on the spot.

Inspirational fuel for your journey

"Knowing YOU inspires a strength that cannot be disputed and confidence that cannot be shaken."

Truly getting to know yourself means that you have an unwavering vision and understanding of how you feel, how you think, what you believe and whom you are. With this knowing, comes a firm stance of conviction regarding all things YOU. This conviction will cause and spark your strength all while igniting your confidence. Knowing YOU is a process of understanding yourself on a deeper level and being willing to explore and embrace what you find.

Action Toward Greatness (ATG):

Start thinking deeply about who you really are!

What is your real personality? (explain)

What are your Core Value?s (morale code)

What are your dreams?

What are your moods/emotions?

What are your likes and dislikes?

How do you feel about your body?

*Now step outside of yourself for a minute

Someone has contacted you requesting that you write a letter and give your input regarding someone you know and this person just met. The new person they need to know about goes by the name (YOU). What would your letter say about your mutual friend (be honest and do not hold back?

"Bask in who you are. After all, no one can be a better you than you."

Acceptance of ourselves is the key to the happiness we say we really want. If you are not spending time getting to know who you are or basking in who you have discovered, you are missing out on an opportunity to show appreciation to one of the most originally created, dynamic persons walking in your world.

Action Toward Greatness (ATG):

Have you made these statements?

I want to meet a genuine person (**YOU**)

I want someone I can trust (**YOU**)

I need someone who has my back (**YOU**)

I could go on and on but I will not. The reality is that the answer has and always will lie in what you think, feel, embrace, acknowledge and appreciate about YOU.

STOP

*Plan an appreciation dinner for yourself (within the next 30 days).

*Make sure the dinner is bigger than how you really feel about you (no two guest dinners here).

* On the invitation, let your guests know they need to bring two written statements expressing what they appreciate about you.

* Have your guest stand and share these statements with everyone.

* Afterwards, collect the **Appreciation Statements™**.

"You're just a *Quote* away from *your* Greatness"

"How you see yourself is a direct result of your belief in your Greatness."

You cannot see what you do not believe. The belief that you have the potential to be great is wrapped in your vision of how you see and appreciate you. If the wonderful qualities and capabilities you possess continue to go unnoticed, than so will your vision of imagining yourself walking in your Greatness.

Action Toward Greatness (ATG):

Take the Appreciation Statements your friends made and begin to read them daily

"Sometimes you need to see and hear how great you are from others before you can see and appreciate it in yourself."

"It feels good when you finally reach the point where you are so secure with who you are, that you no longer apologize for being Great."

There will always be naysayers, no matter how big or small you play in the world. Coming to the realization that no one outside of you should play a major part in your belief of your **Greatness** comes with your continued security of knowing you. The day will come when you stand and let the world know you will shine in your greatness and you have no interest in apologizing for it.

Action Toward Greatness (ATG):

Make a list of 10 great things about you. (feel free to use previous lists from above)

Practice saying them aloud with a firm tone every morning. (You are sending a message to your psyche)

My **Greatness** list:

_____

_____

_____

_____

_____

_____

Inspirational fuel for your journey

My Favorite F Word Is Faith!

"Let your Faith be stronger than your fear."

Stepping out and going after the dreams inside of you, require that you have a belief in you and your God given abilities. Your Faith has to be stronger and more determined than your mind and fear of the unknown. Your faith should be your refuge, your stable ground, your comfort in times of despair. Unlike fear, your faith should never waver. For it is and will always be your calm in the midst of any storm, as long as you believe in your favor and blessings.

Action Toward Greatness (ATG):

Take inventory and examine how strong your faith is.

When I hit hard times or something does not go my way or fall into place I:

_____

_____

_____

_____

How often do you look outside yourself for guidance?

_____

_____

_____

_____

When fear has stopped me from achieving something, I

(call a friend, pray, etc.)

_____

_____

_____

_____

"You're just a *Quote* away from *your* Greatness"

"For times when you have to see it to believe it put your dreams, visions and desires in writing in order to map out your plan."

Write the vision; make it plain upon tablets that he may run that read it (Habakkuk 2:2). Expect many bumps on your journey that can give way to opportunities that have the potential to distract you from your purpose. However, when you have the vision that God has given you written down and specifically detailed, even in times of dismay you will not waver from it. It will always serve as a written guide to pick up right where you left off. On your **Greatness journey** you will encounter many people who will offer to help you with your vision (some well-intentioned, others not so much). When you are clear with the vision God has given you it will not matter who steps in your path, as long as you continue to use the written plan as Gods guide to your destiny.

Action Toward Greatness (ATG):

Has God given you a vision that you have yet to write down? (write it now)

_____

_____

_____

_____

"The path has already been cleared for you. Now go get your blessings."

When you release your faith in big ways, you become open to a glimpse of God's path for you. A momentum that propels you into your purpose rewards each step of faith that you take. Your path was constructed and paved for you long before you were born. To walk into your predestined life requires that you be bold enough to step out on faith and claim what has always been yours. If you have been trying to figure out what to do next, then there lies the problem. You are trying to figure out something that has already been mapped out for you. All you have to do is ask for guidance, and the vision that you have longed to see.

Action Toward Greatness (ATG):

Review what you already know about your path.

Do you have gifts and talents that you feel are calling you to a particular career? (if so, what are they and what career)

_____

_____

_____

_____

Do you feel a constant pull inside of you that you are
ignoring? (if so, what is it)

_____

_____

_____

_____

Have you asked God to reveal your vision and path? (if
not, why)

_____

_____

_____

_____

Inspirational fuel for your journey

"The moment you start to believe you are great, the world won't have a choice but to believe it and receive it."

You were created by a king, which means there is **Greatness** already in your DNA. You must claim it, accept it and believe it as your reality. Just like in the past you have convinced yourself and wrapped your mind around what you cannot be, it is now time to do the same in the opposite direction. Winning is in you and there is nothing left for you to do but to share that winning spirit with the world. You are not a victim; you are a victor who will not accept defeat. Your lineage mandates that you are nothing less than someone who's **Reign** cannot be stopped. You were given dominion over your life and there is nothing the world can do about it. For they have no choice but to accept who you step forward and show yourself to be, which is

GREATNESS BOUND ™.

Action Toward Greatness (ATG):

What message have you given the world about who you

are?

_____

_____

_____

_____

What mental shifts do you need to make in order to represent your Greatness?

_____

_____

_____

_____

What additional knowledge about who you were created to be do you need to learn? (growth is a process)

_____

_____

_____

_____

"You're just a Quote away from your Greatness"

"God has given you all the tools, resources and connections you need to fulfill your dreams. Your doubt is just another time when you have allowed your expectations to over shadow the blessing."

So often, we pray and ask to receive the desires of our heart, yet because they do not come in the form we have envisioned we do not leave ourselves open to receive them. Even worse, we flat out reject them. We must learn that getting in the way or refusing a blessing is equivalent to a starving man making a list and telling us what he will not eat, yet questioning why he is still hungry. Realize that God is the ultimate architect who knows what we need, when we need it and how we need it.

Action Toward Greatness (ATG):

Has there been a times when your prayers were answered

and your blessing were staring you in the face?

Write out a time when you overlooked a blessing because

it did not come in the form you thought it would.

_____

_____

_____

_____

What have you learned from this experience?

_____

_____

_____

_____

Inspirational fuel for your journey

"Faith is not just a word; it is necessary to push you to your highest level."

Many have journeyed to discover their purpose, passion, and **Greatness,** all to find out that when things became too difficult they lacked the necessities to continue. Faith is more than just a word it is the unshakeable belief and trust that you were put here for a bigger reason. The belief that you are a vessel granted the privilege of being used to further the will of God. This faith gives you confidence in times of despair, perspective in situational confusion and vision in times where many lack. It is a priceless gift to behold and without it, you constantly find yourself in a struggle to continue and remain **Loyal to your Greatness™**.

Action Toward Greatness (ATG):

Examine how you can up level your faith.

On a scale from 1 to 10 where would you say your faith ranks?

_____

_____

_____

_____

Is there a situation you need to let go of in order to move toward the future God has for you?

_____

_____

_____

_____

What does it look like to step up your faith?

_____

_____

_____

_____

"You're just a
Quote
away from
y o u r
Greatness"

"You will either do something in Faith or nothing in fear."

My good friend Arnetta Durham once came to me after seeing my **Greatness Potential** and she wanted to know what had me so afraid. I will never forget that conversation as long as I live.

See she was just being obedient to God by asking me the question, but that very question caused me to take a long hard look at myself and finally get real. It was a take no prisoner's kind of conversation.

You know those conversations you can only have with your real friends. She was not going to allow me to squirm my way out of another day of living below my potential, abandoning my God given talents, neglecting my **Greatness** or ignoring the call on my life. God had sent her to do a job. If it meant stepping on my toes or the fall out of our friendship, so be it.

As I searched to put fear into words and share with her, things I had never shared with a living soul. She politely said to me *"God has already equipped you for the vision he has given you, all you need to do is surrender and stop trying to be in control of something you have no control over anyway"*.

"You have already been chosen for this, you don't need to audition". I came up with every excuse I could think of as to why I was not running towards my **Greatness**. Her patience running thin she said listen *"You are either going to do something in faith or nothing in fear"* which is it going to be? Then complete silence came. I thought she had hung up on me so I said *"hello"*.

She replied, *"I am still here waiting on your answer because after you give me your answer that will let me know how I need to pray for you when we get off the phone"*.

I questioned what she meant. She said your answer would tell me if:

1. I need to ask God to strengthen my friend's faith so that she may be strong enough to carry out your will. Or if my prayer will be:

2. *"Lord she is driven by fear and refuses to surrender and get moving. Lord you may want to give that vision to someone who will act on it"*.

Yes, the same look you have on your face I had on mine. It took those words in my face, harsh and strong to make my faith bigger than my fear. I quickly told her to forget the second prayer; I definitely did not want her telling God on me.

That day we prayed, cried, laughed and I shared the visions God had shown me so that she could hold me accountable. There was no turning back after that because as the late Maya Angelou said, "When you know better you do better". Not to mention in that moment I received a glimpse of what life would be like if my purpose belonged to someone else.

It is one thing if I am too fearful to go after it; it is completely something else if it is taken away from me. See that is what we do, we take for granted that the gifts and talents given to us for our purpose will stay intact and always be there whenever we decide to pick them up.

That day I received God's message loud and clear. The one thing I was not going to do was take a chance that the blessings put aside for me would end up given to someone else because I did not rise to the occasion. I knew God had built me better than that and he had brought me through too much for me to turn my back on his plan for me.

That conversation took place in September 2014 and ever since, I have been truly allowing myself to be directed and used by God. I am writing this book today so glad

I DID SOMETHING IN FAITH

Now my question to you is, are you going to do something in Faith or nothing in fear (what will you do)?

_____

_____

_____

_____

Remember You Now Know Better

Inspirational fuel for your journey

Thoughts and Actions!

"When you speak defeat you are saying that you are not worthy of anything more."

Speaking defeat in your life is your way of coming into agreement that you are destined for living beneath your **Greatness**. Sounds harsh, but that is exactly what you are doing. You are saying I am not worthy of anything more than this current stumble. You have accepted it as a part of you, as if it is all you were born to receive.

Action Toward Greatness (ATG):

Practice speaking victory instead of defeat.

I am

_____

_____

_____

_____

I will

_____

_____

_____

_____

"Happiness is a choice made by
those who want it."

There must be a conscious thought to allow you to be happy. Happiness shows up just as often as other emotions do. Therefore, it must be chosen and embraced. You have the power to determine what you will or will not allow in your life. Take that power and make the right decision.

Action Toward Greatness (ATG):

Think about how often different emotions have shown up this week.

Track (tally) which emotions are chosen more often.

Sadness_____

Happiness_____

Frustration_____

Anger_____

Fear _____

Love_____

Reflect back on what led up to the other emotions. Was there room to turn the situation into a happy one?

"Positive thinking infuses energy
into your life."

Positive energy is associated with positive thoughts just as negative energy is in direct relation to negative thoughts. Your thoughts are the seeds of your actions, which will dictate how you react to any given situation. When positivity is the choice, it causes you to see things in your life in a different light. Positivity sparks inspiration, motivation and guides you to explore untapped opportunities.

Action Toward Greatness (ATG):

Are you currently lacking in the area of inspiration and motivation?

If so, a **Positivity Mind Shift** ™ (PMS) is required. Identify what is positive in these areas of your life.

Career

_____

_____

_____

_____

Financial

_____

_____

_____

_____

Reflect on the positivity every time a negative thought comes to mind in these areas.

Family

_____

_____

_____

_____

Personal/Physical

_____

_____

_____

_____

Spiritual

_____

_____

_____

_____

"Positive thinking is recharging your mind and fueling your actions to be more in line with your purpose."

In order to forge towards your purpose, you must have a view of yourself as a person worthy and deserving of that purpose. This does not happen if you are not seeing yourself and your gifts in a positive light. When there is positive thinking, you are resetting the negative information received throughout the day and recharging your outlook on your life. This charge allows you to spring into action and creates a yearning to fulfill your purpose.

Action Toward Greatness (ATG):

Reflection time!

What are you already positive about?

_____

_____

_____

_____

How can you use this towards your purpose?

_____

_____

_____

_____

If you have not discovered your purpose start with thinking about what you are naturally good at doing.

_____

_____

_____

_____

You're just a
Quote
away from
your
Greatness

"Be protective of what you allow to enter your mind and take root. So many times negativity and self-doubt creep in because they were invited."

So often, we will enter a crowded room or befriend individuals' wide open and naïve to the opposition that awaits us. We have to understand that whether on purpose or not, people will say and do things that have the potential to get into our psyche and bump us off our path towards **Greatness**. This is why we must be very selective and protective about those invited into our personal space/inner circle. We must view this space as sacred and to enter you must be highly qualified. To allow access to everyone wanting to enter is like playing Russian roulette with your purpose, calling, and destiny. We should have the perspective that everyone can knock, however access is limited.

Action Toward Greatness (ATG):

Think about how you can prepare and protect your sacred space going forward.

Make a list on your strategy (i.e. prayer etc.)

_____

_____

_____

_____

"When self-doubt creeps in, make sure you remove it before it starts to drain the belief reserve you have built up."

Everyone has a belief foundation that they go to and lean on in good times and bad. If by chance you have allowed anything (including people) to enter your life and as a result you doubt just how **Great** you truly are, it is time to IMMEDIATLEY extract that bug like the leach it is. For if you make the decision to allow it to stay (be very clear it is a decision) it will be left to do what it does best, which is deplete your positivity, self-love, and motivation. A leach is only happy when allowed to get fatter off the lifeline that runs through you.

Action Toward Greatness (ATG):

Take inventory of what or who is draining your belief

reserve.

Make a list of the key drainers.

_____

_____

_____

_____

Make a strategy to extract them (I know it is hard but your Greatness depends on it).

_____

_____

_____

_____

Inspirational fuel for your journey

"Since people cannot literally feel your pain, what makes you think they will be able to see your vision? Discovering your life's purpose is an individual journey; make sure you walk it that way."

As wonderful as taking everyone with you sounds the truth of the matter is that God uniquely created your journey for you. There will be those strategically placed to attend seasons with you, but never confuse it as a superior influence to the vision you have been destined to reveal. It would be a travesty to allow permanent placement of anyone on your path, who alters a vision, not designed for them.

Action Toward Greatness (ATG):

It is time to get honest.

What vision have you been given?

_____

_____

_____

_____

Have you allowed others to alter the original vision?

_____

_____

_____

_____

How can you take the vision back?

_____

_____

_____

_____

You're just a Quote away from your Greatness

"You have the power of choice and it is your obligation to use it to propel you forward in life, not hold you back."

Every choice made in life needs to be carefully analyzed and dissected. Evaluate if it is helping you to walk towards your Greatness or if it is establishing yet another roadblock to your destiny. Do not be disillusioned into thinking that you are not making choices that can affect your journey. Even when you think you are not making a choice, a choice is being made.

Action Toward Greatness (ATG):

Become mindful of your choice process.

Are you more inclined to sit around and let things happen? (Explain)

_____

_____

_____

_____

Do you view decision making as being confrontational?

_____

_____

_____

_____

Is it difficult for you to recognize your power during the
decision making process?

_____

_____

_____

_____

Inspirational fuel for your journey

"Live your life as if you were put
here for a reason."

There are people who sit idly by and watch the lives of others in amazement, as if they are not capable of achieving their own wonder. What you recognize in others you also possess, the only difference is they are making it happen. Life is a precious gift that needs to be unwrapped, used and appreciated. Standing on the sidelines will get you nothing but dirt in your face by those running by.

Action Toward Greatness (ATG):

Reality Check.

Why do you think you are here? (yes this is a real question)

_____

_____

_____

_____

Have there been times when you have felt envious of

someone else's success?

_____

_____

_____

_____

List the characteristics/traits you see in them.

_____

_____

_____

_____

Study those traits. How many of those traits do you
actually possess?

_____

_____

_____

_____

Note: Anything recognized in others (good or bad) is
typically identified because they are in you as well (small
amount or large). This would mean you already possess
what is required to live your purpose.

"Never count yourself out. Your gifts and talents are present for a reason. The world is just waiting for you to have the courage to use them."

There is nothing more defeating than when you tell yourself NO. You do not wait for the answer, you just refuse to try or apply for the opportunity. Do you understand that each gift you have is there for a reason and directly correlates to your purpose? Keeping these gifts and talents hidden away is a display of selfishness. Embrace the gifts designed specifically for you to be shared by you, their intended user. The mere fact that you possess them serves as permission to walk with authority and claim your birthright. STOP walking in fear of what is yours.

Action Toward Greatness (ATG):

Acknowledge what scares you.

Why do you think you have not acted on your gifts/talents?

_____

_____

_____

_____

Is there an insecurity about them, if so why?

_____

_____

_____

_____

What part of your gifts are you secure about?

_____

_____

_____

_____

Prepare yourself to move forward during times when your courage is low.

I will stay strong when

_____

I was given the gift of _____ to share with the world.

"You're just a
Quote
away from
your
Greatness"

"Visualize the life that you want, and then don't stop until your reality mimics your vision."

Everyone has experienced visions and desires for their lives. These visions will replay themselves through the different stages of your journey. When you receive, your vison downloads keep track of them, for they are the blueprint to your future. You must evaluate them and figure out what actions you need to take to make them happen.

Action Toward Greatness (ATG):

Purchase a journal so that you may track your vision.

Inspirational fuel for your journey

Meet Your New Best Friends
Greatness and Dream!

"The only thing holding us back from our Greatness is the belief that it is attainable."

If you truly desire **Greatness**, you must release the doubt that you have been carrying around with you year after year. There comes a time when you have to decide to get out of your own way and take a chance on you. No more telling yourself what you cannot be. From now on, you only speak to yourself about what you can be. Your seeds of **Greatness** are in you and they are just waiting to be cared enough about to be watered.

Action Toward Greatness (ATG):

Ask yourself if you have been standing in your own way.

Without thinking, make a list of what you CAN be.

_____

_____

_____

_____

"Greatness Starts with A State of Mind."

To acquire **Greatness,** you must understand that in order to be great in one's life it requires you to do more than just show up. Showing up will only keep you average. For those who want to go after **Greatness** it requires an over and above state of mind. No holds barred, take no prisoner, and go get it mindset.

It is that cannot sleep, so I am up at two in the morning because I have to get this idea out of my head or else. Greatness requires that you are willing to do what others are not willing to do. It is seeing yourself at your personal best and running towards that vision like a tiger after its prey.

Action Toward Greatness (ATG):

Analyzation time

Do you see yourself as living average or **Greatness?**

_____

_____

_____

_____

How would you say you have been living so far?

_____

_____

_____

_____

Describe how you can elevate your current living to fall in
line with your vision.

_____

_____

_____

_____

You're just a
Quote
away from
your
Greatness

"Greatness is a mindset not a label. So don't let anyone tell you that you can't afford to possess it."

The misconception many have about living their Greatness is that it is only for a select few and not for them. This is simply not true. Although Beyoncé speaks about wearing expensive purple labels in her song "upgrade u" that many of us cannot yet afford, **Greatness** is one priceless treasure we all have access too. So in life never allow anyone to make you feel that your seed of greatness does not deserve to be cultivated the same as anyone else's.

Action Towards Greatness (ATG):

Begin thinking of yourself as worthy (of all things).

"Never give up on the dreams that have been created inside of you. The day you become aware of them is the day they become a part of who you are."

Once your dreams have revealed themselves to you, they become your moral obligation to see them to reality. You can try to deny your purpose and refuse to walk the path that was designed for you however, be prepared for the price that comes with that denial. Many have looked back on their lives and not recognized what they see. All that is left is a life laced with a plethora of regrets instead of ReGreats.

Action Toward Greatness (ATG):

Embrace your dreams

"We never doubted your gifts or your talents. We are just waiting for you to have the courage to share them."

Repeatedly we come across individuals who will compliment us on gifts and talents that we say are no big deal. Time after time, others recognize in us what we do not see in ourselves. We brush it off by saying, "Oh you're so nice", which simply is not true. They are not saying it because they want to be nice, they cannot help but acknowledge it. The real reason why you are brushing it off is that deep down inside you know, to acknowledge it would cause them to look at you with the expectation of you doing something with it.

Action Toward Greatness (ATG):

Past Recall time.

Have there been times when you have blown off compliments?

_____

_____

_____

_____

Have you ever asked yourself why?

_____

_____

_____

_____

Tell yourself why you think it is that you reacted that way.

_____

_____

_____

_____

Are we avoiding the expectations of others?

Inspirational fuel for your journey

"Master your purpose and defeat your doubt"

The more prepared you are the more confident you tend to feel. Now, do not mistake this, as permission to beat preparation in the ground but it is a simple "I get it". If you doubt your gifts and talents, you need to get busy doing something about it. Just like the day, you learned to ride a bike without training wheels it required you to get on the bike first. As time went on you became more comfortable and confident with every step forward.

The same rings true with your gifts. The more you step out and acquire knowledge to enhance them, the more you are empowered to share them (Note: not only book knowledge).

Action Toward Greatness (ATG):

LET'S GET GOING!

"Don't let another day go by that you are not walking in your Greatness. It is not about how big or small the step, all that matters is that you keep moving."

The willingness to spring into action is the number one component needed to achieve the **Greatness** that awaits you. Resist becoming stagnant or intimidated by the result. The saying is true "You can only eat an elephant one piece at a time" and the same goes for your dreams.

There may be many things required of you before the dream is completely fulfilled however, the most important one starts with you putting one foot in front of another.

Action Toward Greatness (ATG):

Assess your **Great-Ability**

I am great.

_____

_____

_____

What steps can I take right now to move me forward?

_____

_____

_____

"You are the only ruler that should measure your Greatness."

You put your fate in the hands of others when you allow them to dictate what part you play in your **Greatness**. You received a specific assignment that comes with an embedded restlessness that alerts you when it is time to enlarge your vision. It is that *"I have to do more because I am no longer satisfied with my life"* feeling.

Later it turns into *"I need to make some changes or I am going to scream"* feeling. See without this restless alarm going off you would be completely ok with where you are in your life right now.

This uniquely designed alarm was created and set for your Greatness Table. You are the receiver of your **Greatness Download,** so only you can measure the steps in which you rule.

Action Toward Greatness (ATG):

Create your **Greatness** table.

Greatness Ideas	Greatness Start Date	Greatness Action	Greatness Completion Date

"Make sure you always chart your journey, so that in times of doubt you can look back and see how far you've come, how good you already are and how great you are destined to be."

One of the worst things you can do when you are striving for **Greatness** is to lose touch with your journey. Staying connected to the progress is a pivotal component in helping you tap into your "stick to it" reserves. When you are able to see that you are growing and transforming into a **Greatness Conqueror** it unleashing a newfound energy and brings about the mindset needed to continue. You take on that "Can't stop, Won't stop, Couldn't stop if I wanted to" drive.

Action Towards Greatness (ATG):

Chart your journey/progress

My **Greatness** Journey (list your truth)

| |
| |
| |
| |

"One of the greatest moments in your life will be the day you walk into the Greatness that has always been waiting for you."

A true reveal occurs in your life the day you realize that you too have seeds of **Greatness** placed inside of you. Not only are they where they have always been, but it is not too late for you to unmask your true purpose, spread your wings and soar like the eagle you were destined to be.

Action Towards Greatness (ATG):

Think of yourself as that soaring eagle.

"Listen to the voices that keep speaking inside of you. They belong to your best friends Greatness and Dream. They will keep calling until you answer."

You hear whispers but you do not respond. You feel a pull but you do not know where it is coming from. These are your friends **Greatness** and **Dream** trying to tell you it is time for you to walk into the life you were meant to live.

Everything you have envisioned can be your reality if you will just answer your calling. You may not know how but they are telling you do not worry about that part.

They are letting you know it is time to let go of what has been holding you back, what has caused you to not live up to your potential.

Release those who say you cannot do it. **Greatness** and **Dream** are friends that will stick by you but you have to want them as much as they want you.

"If you do not go after your dreams with laser focus, then you cannot get mad at your scattered results."

Once you have decided to answer the call of **Greatness** and **Dream,** you must go after them with vigor so focused that it is unshakable. There is a danger that persists if you approach them with a passive lackadaisical attitude.

They will fall to the sideline or worse the background as other things have done. Ultimately, you will find yourself missing your true calling and purpose.

Your commitment to your **Greatness** will eventually wheeled great results. However, a lack of laser focus and commitment bring about results that are inconsistent and will cause major frustration on your journey. This is a very toxic place to be since many will opt to give up during this self-imposed difficult time.

Action Toward Greatness (ATG):

Set a daily reminder on your phone of what it would mean for you to achieve your dreams. Every day that it notifies you think of it as your pledge of commitment to see that dream come to reality.

Inspirational fuel for your journey

Distractions Be Dammed!

**"Remove all things that impede
your journey to Greatness."**

A major reason our Greatness often escapes us is the lack of a flourishing environment. We cannot expect dreams to grow in a toxic atmosphere. It is cleaning time and for the sake of our **Greatness,** we are taking no prisoners.

Just like a refrigerator that needs constant cleaning or the things inside will begin to stink and decay, so does our mind and personal space when toxic things linger around. Anything or anyone standing in the way of our **Greatness** must move to the sideline of our path.

We do not have time to jump over them because at this point we have allowed them to hold us back for too long. Its go time and that means "**AINT NOBODY GOT TIME FOR THAT**".

Action Toward Greatness (ATG):

Time to make some decisions

Make a list of things that are positive in your life. (job, school etc.)

_____

_____

_____

_____

List people and things that you feel would be a distraction or negative. Be truthful about whom and what needs sidelining.

_____

_____

_____

_____

If you could only save 3 people in your world who would they be and why?

_____

_____

_____

_____

These people are your Greatness Team (those you can count on to lift you up when you are struggling).

_____

_____

_____

_____

You're just a
Quote
away from
your
Greatness

"On your journey to Greatness make a conscious decision to monitor who you allow in your space."

Once you have cleaned up existing distractions that you allowed to hang around, hang on and hold up your Greatness. It is pivotal that you do not allow any new toxic carriers to enter into your space. This is the time when you want to be careful with whom you share your time, thoughts and dreams. Protect them as if they are your newborn babies.

They are precious, vulnerable and need your unwavering guard. Be willing to lay yourself on the line for them, because in the end you will see that they are in fact the reason your entire life has lined up the way it has.

They are the real reason you breathe the air you breathe. Their survival is detrimental to you understanding their purpose in your destiny.

Action Towards Greatness (ATG):

Devise a strategy for handling new toxic people and situations.

What will you say?

_____

_____

_____

_____

What actions will you take?

_____

_____

_____

_____

This is also a good time to ramp up your visualization exercise so that the dream never leaves your sight.

_____

_____

_____

_____

Inspirational fuel for your journey

"A dream deferred do to life's obstacles is a dream that was never believed in."

Life just happens and there is no changing that fact. There are simply things that are out of your control and to try would be taking on a foolish task. The question is not if something will happen it is when something will happen. There can be chaos all around but that does not have to mean you abandon your dreams.

Challenges are a part of your personal growth and testimony. Without them, you would remain stuck as the person you started out to be. Without them, you would never appreciate the good times. You would never push yourself to conquer and dig deep to overcome. Begin to ask yourself, are you going to sacrifice the life of your babies (i.e. dreams) because things are not perfect?

Many things have been born inside of great people during the toughest times of their lives (books, songs, inventions, etc.). Therefore, any thought of you giving up and throwing in the towel is only you doubting yourself and using it as an excuse.

Up to this point, you have given many reasons why your dreams have gone unpursued. If given the opportunity, I am sure you can come up with enough reasons to last the rest of your life. This is a time to acknowledge what has been in front of you for years. **YOU STILL DOUBT THE DREAM**.

Not that they are not good enough or that they will not work but instead that you are not worthy and deserving of this magnificent gift. With this internal sabotage on the horizon, it is very important that you recognize and destroy it on sight.

Get very clear, about who you are in this moment. Resist falling back into the old patterns that have had you shackled all your life. You are not only worthy but you have been specifically chosen for this dream. Without you there is no dream and without dream there is only a shell of the real and true you.

Action Toward Greatness (ATG):

Become pattern resistant.

I Believe

_____

_____

_____

_____

I AM worthy of

_____

_____

_____

_____

I will not allow myself to

_____

_____

_____

_____

I Believe I was called to

_____

_____

_____

_____

"Don't stop moving forward. It is not the obstacles that keep us from our greatness and dreams it's the lack of action."

The longer you sit around and ponder your world and its many turns, the longer you live a dream-deferred life. Even with the weight of the world on you, do not you dare stop moving.

I sit here today writing this book in hopes that it will help someone in the world, all while next to my mother in the hospital as she receives her five-hour chemotherapy treatments.

Many completion deadlines have come and gone but it does not matter. I understand that in this current fight it is not about when it is complete but that it is completed.

If this recent obstacle requires me to take time to care for my mother without a doubt It will happen, because she comes first (She is also one of my Greatness Team Members).

As long as I do not stop and keep moving on my journey to **Greatness,** I am still fulfilling my destiny. Any time I even think about giving up or stopping I ask myself *"how do I tell her to keep going, never give up and fight for her life"* if I am so quick to give up on something that is not nearly as challenging.

So ask yourself, are those obstacles really "Dream Deferred Worthy"?

Action Toward Greatness (ATG):

As current obstacles come your way access if they are

Dream Deferred Worthy.

Don't You Dare Dim Your Light

"When you dim your light you are inviting darkness and confusion inside of you."

Many have gone through life lost and constantly in search of themselves. Impart because they have dimmed their light so much to accommodate others that it has become a flicker.

Where there is no light there is darkness and where there is darkness there is a lack of vision. There is no ability to see or discover what is inside, when you keep diming the light lit within.

Your internal light brings clarity and direction. It keeps you from stumbling and bumping into things. More importantly, it keeps you from going down the wrong path do to that lack of vision.

Those who cannot see in front of them are hesitant to move or take the necessary steps on their **Greatness Path**. The reason this time can be so detrimental at this point of your process is that you are starting to bloom and open up.

That means you are shining and others see it. Especially those we spoke of earlier who were placed on the sideline. So do not be surprised if the very people you thought would be happy for you will show no emotion what so ever about your newfound **Greatness Run**.

You must not alter how you walk your walk to make them feel better about what you are doing. If you do, you risk inviting darkness and losing your way permanently.

#AINT NOBODY WORTH THAT

Action Toward Greatness (ATG):

Make a promise to yourself that you will put you before those that cannot handle your **Greatness**.

I PROMISE as of this date (write it out in full):

_____

_____

_____

_____

"You're just a *Quote* away from *your* Greatness"

"Don't look at the results of others as a barometer for judging when you shine."

Never let what someone else is doing determine when you shine. Your journey is tailor made, therefore when consumed with looking over at another person's path you overlook key details left on your own.

Your path and current growth go hand in hand, so it is useless to look at what others are doing with anything but admiration and motivation.

Truthfully speaking, if you were there right now you would not be able to handle it. The necessary tools and stamina needed to win that race have not been developed in you just yet. It is called your time for a reason.

Enjoy the learning and growing so that you are undoubtedly prepared for your **Greatness.** Savor collecting the pebbles on your path, for they will wheeled you the skills, experience and weapons you need to prosper.

"When you dim your light you are telling yourself you are not worthy of the shine that has been placed in you."

You have the power to reinforce the positive or negative feelings that you have experienced. **Greatness** requires reaching deep past those emotions and pulling from reserves you did not even know you had. You were meant to be great and that means you shine just by being who you are.

You actually go against your true make up when you dim your light. That shine is upon you because it is your gift cheering you on and telling you to keep going. It is your gift telling you, we have this, do not give up.

It is your gift telling you, do not believe the doubt, you are worthy. In those tempting times when you feel like diming your light, keep in mind that in that moment you are succumbing to the negative thoughts of unworthiness.

Action Toward Greatness (ATG):

Monitor and Track the times when you are allowing your feelings of unworthiness to creep in. It takes practice to train your mind to debunk years of habit. Do not worry, it will happen and the more you acknowledge it the easier it becomes.

Tracking your feelings, (I felt unworthy when).

_____

_____

_____

_____

This caused me to dim my light (How).

_____

_____

_____

_____

Inspirational fuel for your journey

"When you take your Greatness for granted, you run the risk of your Greatness not showing up when you need it."

Diming your light repeatedly jeopardizes the strength of your **Greatness**. Just as a lantern is constantly turned down, there will be times when your light will go out completely.

You have taken for granted that it will always be there when you need it. That simply is not the case. The light is your inner hype person better known as your SHE-HYPE ™ (or HE-Hype ™) and they cheer you on and propel you forward.

They magnify and celebrate your **Greatness** and stand up to fear on your behalf. They require your loyalty because if they are neglected or taken for granted they become weak and unable to hold you up.

Just like an athlete training for their craft your **Greatness** needs that same training and loyalty from you.

Action Toward Greatness (ATG):

Exercise your She-Hype™/ He-Hype

1. How many times last week did you allow your inner hype to shine and promote your **Greatness**?

_____

_____

_____

_____

2. How many times did you dim your light last week (what were the circumstances)?

_____

_____

_____

_____

This week you are barred from dimming your light.
You must allow it to become strong and thrive.
Be very in tuned with how easy or difficult it is to refrain from shrinking when given the opportunity.
Pay very close attention to your natural patterns.
The more you know and recognize the inner workings of your psyche, the more you will be able to uncover the triggers that cause you to want to play small when you should be shining.

You're just a *Quote* away from *your* Greatness

Inspirational fuel for your journey

"Shine At All Times"

Your ability to shine is one that lies within your inner child. It is that spark that you were born with, that initial untapped seed of **Greatness** that was placed inside of you. It is that seed in its purest form, before the world told you what you could not do and who you could not become. It resides in the space that you have reserved for your eyes only. However, just like you have come of age on the outside the time has come for you to finally heal from all those negative experiences, and walk into the **Greatness** that has always been you!

"Your Greatness is a precious commodity that should always be searched for, cultivated, polished and displayed" Lisa Guice

Conclusion

There is no quick overnight solution for the many years that you have run from your Greatness. Like with anything in life the process of change can be a difficult one if you have not made up your mind to **Be Loyal To Your Greatness** ™ and loyal to the process. The power to pull out what has been there all along resides in your willingness to get honest with yourself and embrace the struggles you have gone through.

Those struggles are not deemed as obstacles or barricades. Their purpose is to strengthen and prepare you for the ultimate reward that has been waiting for your embrace. Whatever your story is, it is to be valued and shared to help others with their journey. No more are you allowed to run and hide from the **Greatness** that has called you from birth or comforted you through the most difficult times.

No longer will you cower against your adversities or be afraid to conquer your mountains. Today, realize that you are unstoppable and

You're Just a Q.U.O.T.E away from your Greatness.

Q= Quit

U= Using

O= Obstacles

T= To

E= Escape your Greatness!

So now, when you look back over your life reflect thankfully for every tear that you have shed on your journey. It's those tears that have brought you to this point mentally, emotionally, and spiritually, where you will no longer settle for anything less than the **Greatness** that has been set aside specifically for you. Realize that those tears served as the water needed to help your seeds of **Greatness** take root, grow and get ready to blossom.

From this very moment, there is an obligation to step outside of your comfort zone because you have officially been stretched to live your life as someone who understands and believes

You're Just a Q.U.O.T.E away from your Greatness

Q = Quit making excuses

U = Use your trails and experiences as your earned degree

O = Own your gifts (don't shy away from them)

T = Take a leap of faith

E = Embrace Your Greatness

"Walking in your **Greatness** is your obligation, not your option." - Lisa Guice

About The Author

Lisa Guice is the CEO of **Lisa Guice Global Vision, LLC** and Founder of **Prettie Girl™** (PG), one of several divisions within **Prettie Girl Enterprises, LLC**. After noticing a lack of positive images in the media and a decline in her daughter's self-esteem due to being the target of bullying she made a life shift. With the support of her family she left her eighteen-year career at a top telecommunications company and embarked on a journey to live out her true passion of uplifting others and teaching them how to solidify a positive relationship with the most valuable person there is, YOU. Understanding that how we feel about ourselves will continue to be the basis of what we attract to us, she developed empowering workshops and programs teaching girls and women how to walk into their greatness and power.

After her group work with multiple women she created a much-needed women's division called **Women Reign Network™** that provides a sisterhood and focuses on empowering women to move from their Pain, to Purpose, and into their Power™ in their lives and businesses.

In addition, Lisa is the creator of the successful Be Great Now™ coaching program and her continued service led her to become a Self-Relationship Expert ™, Author, Inspirational Motivational Speaker, Certified Life Coach, Certified Bully Prevention Specialist, Empowerment and Self-Esteem Building Specialist.

"A woman who knows her power can empower a girl in need ™"

-Lisa Guice-

Lisa Guice Global-Vision, LLC&

Prettie Girl Enterprises, LLC

22424 S Ellsworth Loop Rd #542
Queen Creek AZ, 85142
480-257-4475

Services Available

- Self-Esteem Building Workshops
- Empowerment Camps
- Bully Prevention Camps (for girls)
- Bully Prevention Training (for Parents and School Administrators)
- 1 on 1 Coaching (for Women in life and business)
- Group Coaching (for Women in life and business)
- Seminars & Workshops (for Women desiring **Greatness**)
- Inspirational Motivational Speaking (Schools, Churches, Women's group, Companies and Organizations etc.)

Signature Speaking Topics

Don't You Dare Dim Your light: learn how to identify when you are playing small and the price you pay for not living beyond your comfort zone and insecurities.

5 Steps to Claim Your Greatness No Matter What: Master the ability to use every obstacle in your life as the training ground to stay on your destined path and walk into your Greatness despite the detour signs.

For Booking, Questions or to work with Lisa:

Connect with Lisa Guice:

Facebook, Twitter, Instagram
For All Social Media Please use:
@iamlisaguice
@prettiegirltm

Email: *lgglobalvision@gmail.com*

Visit *http://www.lisaguice.com*

Phone:
480-257-4475

You Can Be Great Now

You know that there is **Greatness** in you but for some reason it has been allowed to lay dormant year after year. Something always holds you back and you do not understand why? Many people allow fear and painful experiences to block them from seeing their potential. This does not have to be you. Lisa Guice trusted Self Relationship Expert™ and creator of Be Great Now™ coaching program will empower you to

* believe you possess Greatness
* stop denying yourself the life you desire
* overcome thoughts of unworthiness
* identify the real obstacles standing in your way
* experience your power to release Greatness Blockers

Are you ready to stop standing in your own way? Today is the day you unleash the life you have been destined, prepared, and created to live?

Lisa Guice helps people discover their true selves and walk into their Greatness. As a Self-Relationship Expert™ and coach she has created empowerment programs, helped clients achieve their dreams and is the founder of Be Great Now Academy (BGNA).